BRITAIN'S RAILWAYS IN THE 1970s

David Hayes

First published 2019

Amberley Publishing
The Hill, Stroud
Gloucestershire, GL5 4EP

www.amberley-books.com

Copyright © David Hayes, 2019

The right of David Hayes to be identified as the Author of this work has been asserted in accordance with the Copyrights, Designs and Patents Act 1988.

ISBN 978 1 4456 8557 1 (print)
ISBN 978 1 4456 8558 8 (ebook)

All rights reserved. No part of this book may be reprinted or reproduced or utilised in any form or by any electronic, mechanical or other means, now known or hereafter invented, including photocopying and recording, or in any information storage or retrieval system, without the permission in writing from the Publishers.

British Library Cataloguing in Publication Data.
A catalogue record for this book is available from the British Library.

Origination by Amberley Publishing.
Printed in the UK.

Appointed GPSR EU Representative: Easy Access System Europe Oü, 16879218
Address: Mustamäe tee 50, 10621, Tallinn, Estonia
Contact Details: gpsr.requests@easproject.com, +358 40 500 3575

Introduction

The 1970s was a unique period for Britain's railways. Steam had not long been replaced by diesel traction, the West Coast Main Line electrification project was well underway with new and more powerful locomotives offering faster journey times, and the colourful rail-blue livery projected an image of a new and altogether cleaner railway. In short, there was plenty to be optimistic about.

It was also a good time for the railway photographer. Much of the railway infrastructure and complex track layouts of the steam era remained intact, and freight traffic was varied, plentiful, and generally passed through one of the several marshalling yards dotted around the country for sorting prior to onward dispatch to the customer. There were also plenty of locomotive classes of various shapes and sizes, often regionally based, to pique the interest of both the photographer and the trainspotter.

However, during this decade the seeds were already being sown for an altogether different railway: one where locomotive standardisation was being pursued as a means of lowering fleet maintenance costs and simplifying driver training; one where the future of freight was no longer seen as wagon-load but the more economical train-load travelling from supplier to customer directly, thus avoiding the inevitable delay and expense of handling in the marshalling yards; and one where track layouts were being simplified and streamlined to increase line speed and reduce permanent way maintenance costs.

The photographs in this book attempt to capture a flavour of the railways during this fascinating transition period.

Born in Nottingham in the mid-1950s, I was exposed early on to the sight, sound and smell of steam traction passing through Beeston station, handily just a few hundred yards from the family home. With an extensive network of collieries in North Nottinghamshire, and plenty of power stations in the Trent Valley, it would be no surprise that coal dominated the freight traffic in the area, with loaded trains often queuing up in the several passing loops waiting for a slot to gain access to Toton Yard. I would be sat on the station footbridge at every opportunity watching all this unfold and, listening to the bells and levers being thrown in the signal box, it was almost inevitable that I would develop a fascination for trains and number collecting.

Steam traction gradually gave way to diesels and some of these, such as the ill-fated Claytons on test from their Derbyshire manufacturers, or the Blue Pullman on its middle of the day out-and-back trip from London to Nottingham, proved to be highlights and stayed in the memory of this eight-year-old lad longer than most of the steam locomotives ever did!

With a growing interest in photography I acquired my first camera, a Kodak Instamatic, when I was eleven years old. However, I was still more interested in collecting numbers at the time and, on reflection, had neither the wisdom nor financial means to take the opportunities the camera offered. The shots that I did take were generally poor but one image did make it into this book – a much-valued one at Mablethorpe station taken during a family holiday.

By my mid-teens, with several long-distance trainspotting trips under my belt, and having witnessed a few first-generation diesel classes already withdrawn, the idea of trying to capture the railway scene on film became more appealing. With a weekend shelf-stacking job at a local supermarket bringing in some extra money, I now had the means to indulge the interest.

My first 'proper' camera was a hand-me-down from my father, an Agfa Billy Zero folding job. Of 1930s vintage, it offered little in the way of luxuries, but using it for a few months in early 1973 gave me the perfect grounding in the technical side of photography. With just eight images per film and a questionable focusing distance calibration, the camera had its limitations and later that year I bought a 35 mm Zenit E, seemingly the 'rite of passage' camera for folks of a certain age. This was swiftly followed by a Praktica L to allow for both colour and black and white photography.

One or two other camera upgrades followed over the next couple of years before full-time employment and a healthier cashflow allowed me to upgrade to a pair of Nikkormat FT2s with 35 mm, 50 mm, 105 mm, and 200 mm fixed focal length lenses. The majority of colour images appearing in this book are scans from Agfa CT18 transparencies, a film that's received a mixed press over the years but, in combination with the Nikon lenses, has produced results that work for me. The monochrome images in the book were mostly taken on Ilford FP4 film and developed in Acutol. The 125 ASA rating is slow by today's standards but careful scanning can tease out a surprising level of shadow detail.

I haven't placed the images in any particular order but rather tried to present them in a way that appeals to me. I hope you enjoy what you see!

David Hayes
April 2019

Class 47 No. 47539 stands under the floodlights in the early hours of a wet night at Crewe, awaiting signals. I almost didn't bother with the photograph, thinking the loco would move off by the time I'd set up the tripod, but I had time to capture one 23-second exposure – and receive a good soaking! I'm now pleased I did, seeing as it's one of my all-time favourites. 21 January 1978.

An overnighter at Crewe in the 1970s was always rewarding given the volume of traffic, especially seeing as almost everything stopped, thus becoming a snapping opportunity. In this shot Class 86 No. 86002, captured on a 50-second exposure, stands with a northbound parcels working. 21 January 1978.

When this shot was taken the writing was already on the wall for the first batch of Peaks to enter BR service. Seen here at Cheadle Hulme in weather reflecting the mood of the event, Peak No. 44009 *Snowdon* is hauling the 'Farewell to the Class 44s' enthusiasts' special. 21 January 1978.

Emerging from Brush's Loughborough workshops in 1961 as their answer to BR's need for lightweight second-generation diesels, the twin-engined D0280 *Falcon* was obsolete almost immediately given advances in diesel technology making single power plants feasible. Now renumbered 1200 and relegated to occasional local trip workings, *Falcon* passes through Newport station a year before withdrawal. 19 April 1974.

On a sunny July evening, a pair of BRC&W Class 26s stand at Inverness with trains to the extremities of the Scottish railway system. On the right No. 26032 is heading the 5.15 p.m. to Thurso and Wick and, on the left, No. 26023 stands with the 5.45 p.m. to Kyle of Lochalsh. 22 July 1977.

With the summer timetable now in operation, a pair of Class 31s – Nos 31308 and 31244 – bask in the sunlight as they approach Leicester beneath the wonderful array of semaphores. This class regularly performed on the Norwich–Birmingham trains at the time, but in fact these two were working the summer-timetabled Yarmouth–Walsall service. 27 May 1978.

Breaking out of the shadows just in time for the photographer, Class 31 No. 31216 hurries the 8.05 a.m. Birmingham–Norwich service through Melton Mowbray. The introduction of loco-hauled trains would likely have been welcomed by passengers, who had been more used to travelling this lengthy route on DMUs. 1 October 1977.

When this shot was taken, Oban station was still largely intact with its elegant glazed roof. To complete the scene, a pair of BRC&W Class 27s – Nos 27003 and 27043 – stand with the 5.45 p.m. service to Glasgow Queen Street. The vehicles in the foreground are queuing for one of the local ferry services. 18 July 1977.

In wintry conditions a pair of Class 31s – Nos 31246 and 31227 – leave the East Coast Main Line at Newark with a ballast train and take the freight-only Great Northern branch towards Bottesford. The branch, once part of a wider system extending to Leicester and Northampton, saw little traffic and was closed altogether in 1988. 6 January 1979.

This shot captures Sulzer No. 25216 throwing up some smoke as she accelerates up the grade out of St Austell, heading west towards Truro. Almost as interesting as the loco are the three cars in the station car park – believed to be a Datsun Cherry, Austin A70 and a Hillman Minx. 21 July 1976.

A warm spring evening sees a pair of Class 20s – Nos 20090 and 20170 (the latter still in BR green livery) – rattling their way north through Toton Yard with returning coal empties. The hump reception lines in the background look unusually bare, a sign of the slow but inexorable transition towards block payload freight trains. 20 May 1977.

A pair of Sulzer Class 25s – Nos 25065 and 25062 – roll into Newtonmore with the 10.05 Glasgow Queen Street–Inverness service. Interesting to note is the smart uniform of the station official, who appears to be waiting to put a package on board. 23 July 1977.

Making its way south through Newtonmore is Class 40 No. 40063, working the 12.10 Inverness–Edinburgh. Unsurprisingly there's little going on in the goods yard, although it appears coal deliveries are still being made. The signal box was switched out of use on this visit. 23 July 1977.

From the gloomy, spartan interior that defined Mirfield station in the 1970s comes a brief ray of hope for the railway photographer in the form of Class 40 No. 40156, seen heading east with a passing freight. This is one of my favourite monochrome shots from the period. 12 April 1977.

A tidy scene at Wickford sees a pair of four-car AM7 EMUs departing with a Great Eastern service from Liverpool Street to Southend Victoria. The signal box was in operation when this shot was taken, and the station was (and still is) the junction for the Southminster branch, which was DMU-operated at the time. 5 September 1976.

Peaks were the predominant motive power on the Midland Main Line and, captured passing through Beeston with a rake of Mark 1 carriage stock, is No. 45030 hauling the 16.05 Nottingham–St Pancras service. On the left is the old goods shed, long closed when this shot was taken, and still standing in 2018. 2 October 1977.

More commonly associated with freight traffic, the Class 20s were occasionally put to other duties. In this instance No. 20002 is acting as station pilot and is captured setting off from Glasgow Central with the empty stock of the 7.15 a.m. service from Nottingham. I'd arrived on this train myself to start a week-long Scottish Rail Rover. 26 August 1978.

There's nothing like the sound of levers being thrown, the clank of pegs and the ting-ting coming from the signal box. Even with the doors shut against a bitingly cold frost, all this could still be heard at the end of Wellingborough Up platform on 10 December 1976. In the meantime, adding a backing track all of its own, Sulzer No. 25125 gurgles away as it shunts coal wagons back into the yard.

Class 37 No. 37186 stands at Bristol Temple Meads in the early hours after arriving with a mail and parcels service from Swansea. When the Post Office staff complete their work, the train will return to South Wales as the 1.24 a.m. to Milford Haven. The train usually included a couple of carriages for late-traveling passengers. 15 April 1978.

Peak No. 45119 stands at Nottingham with an early morning service to London St Pancras. Barely visible above the engine is the girder bridge that carried the old Great Central line into Nottingham Victoria. The bridge was removed a few years later only to be replaced with a new structure for the Nottingham tramway system. 20 November 1976.

Sulzer No. 25194 approaches Meadow Lane foot crossing, midway between Attenborough and Beeston stations, with a Freightliner train destined for the Nottingham Terminal located a couple of miles down the track. The train had likely originated from the Dudley Terminal. 9 February 1978.

Still sporting green livery, a pair of Class 20s – Nos 20152 and 20175 – head north at Syston South Junction with a mixed freight. I never look at this shot without wondering what happened to the family on the left, nor if they knew they had the perfect spot for an allotment. 8 June 1977.

The last day of Class 52 working was marked with a double-headed excursion, the 'Western Tribute', seen here hauled by No. 1023 *Western Fusilier* and No. 1013 *Western Ranger* as it passes Cardiff. Keen to get away from the masses, four of us walked out west from the station and found this spot, conveniently near The Cottage, a local hostelry where we commemorated their passing. 26 February 1977.

The delightful Newton-on-Ayr station features in this shot, and pictured here is Sulzer No. 25090 bringing in what is thought to be a rake of redundant NCB internal-user wagons from the recently closed Pennyvenie Colliery. The line to the docks and Falkland Yard is on the left. 30 August 1978.

Introduced in 1960 as part of the West Coast Main Line electrification programme, the slam-door Class 304s provided an adequate, if not especially comfortable, ride for commuters. In this shot unit No. 011 comes off the Stoke-on-Trent loop into Cheadle Hulme with a service to Manchester Piccadilly. 21 January 1978.

The Liverpool–Newcastle route was one of the last strongholds for passenger haulage by the much-loved Class 40s, and in this shot No. 40017 draws into Huddersfield with one such train. Interesting to see one of the carriage doors opening before the train has come to a stop – something now unheard of with today's central locking systems. 12 April 1977.

Coal traffic heading south to London from Toton Yard was still plentiful in the 1970s, and one such train is captured passing Wellingborough under clear signals on a bitterly cold December morning in the hands of Peak No. 45058. 10 December 1976.

Deltic No. 55006 *The Fife and Forfar Yeomanry* hustles the 'The Aberdonian' (12.15 ex-King's Cross) down Stoke Bank and out of the mist at Grantham in the presence of a few 'extras'. The well-camouflaged one acknowledging the photographer has just arrived, quite possibly on a shift change. 1 May 1978.

Passengers and trainspotters alike stop to admire the sight of Class 47 No. 47500 powering through the centre road at Reading with the 12.40 p.m. Weston-super-Mare – London Paddington service. No franchises, coffee shops or eateries adorn the platform in this view – how times have changed. 13 July 1974.

Pushing the boundaries of the film, Peak No. 45075 hauls the well-loaded evening Freightliner to York, where the train will be split into Coatbridge, Edinburgh and Newcastle portions. This train was a regular runner from the Nottingham Terminal and typically passed this spot, the Meadow Lane foot crossing near Beeston, around 7.15 p.m. 6 May 1977.

A visit to the Castle Keep was essential for any photographer wanting to snap trains running over the complex diamond crossings at the eastern end of Newcastle station. This lucky shot sees Class 37 No. 37058 passing with a short freight as Deltic No. 55016 *Gordon Highlander* heads north with an unidentified Anglo-Scottish express. 8 September 1976.

Against a backdrop of steel mills, Peak No. 46053 rounds the curve from Sheffield under clear signals and approaches the old Rotherham (Masboro) station with a south-west to north-east route working. The area has undergone significant change with the decline of UK steelmaking and the yard, at one time busy enough to support a pair of shunters, no longer exists. 16 September 1977.

Railway enthusiasts would appreciate the fine view from the back bedrooms of these houses on Swaddale Avenue, Chesterfield. In this shot Peak No. 45101 approaches the station with the 9.35 a.m. Carlisle–Nottingham service. Judging by the backyards I'm guessing it was washing day. 20 August 1977.

Less than 5 miles into a journey of over 500 miles, an as yet unnamed Class 50 No. 50011 coasts down the grade into Par with the thinly patronised (on this day at least) St Austell–Stirling Motorail service. 21 July 1976.

Shortly after 7 p.m., and against the backdrop of Nottingham city centre some 3 miles distant, Peak No. 45050 edges out of the Freightliner Terminal at Beeston with the 4E62 working to York. Here it will be split into Coatbridge, Edinburgh and Newcastle portions and will be marshalled into other trains heading to those destinations. 17 May 1977.

With the steam-heating apparatus working well, Deltic No. 55012 *Crepello* waits in the small hours at York station with a sleeper train believed to be the 10.15 p.m. King's Cross–Aberdeen, 'The Night Aberdonian'. Night shots were more appealing with the cab-light on, and the driver kindly agreed to the request on this occasion. 4 February 1978.

On a less than summery Saturday, where even the level crossing attendant has decided to take refuge in his hut, Class 47 No. 47106 takes the through road at Exeter St Davids with the 8.10 a.m. Leeds–Paignton service. 12 July 1975.

One of my personal favourite photographs sees a Derby-twin Class 114 DMU at Holmes Junction with a service to Sheffield shortly after leaving Rotherham Masborough. The backdrop of terrace houses, oil tankers in the sidings and Millmoor football stadium floodlights epitomize the South Yorkshire scene for me in the 1970s. 16 September 1977.

Good weather days on the Woodhead Route were always welcomed, but arranging a day off work to coincide with one could be tricky. I struck lucky here though, and Class 76 No. 76001 is seen drifting down the grade at Hadfield with a coal train, against an autumnal Pennine backdrop. 17 November 1977.

An everyday station scene in the 1970s, when mailbags were left unattended on platform trolleys, ready to be loaded on to the train that would take them to their next destination. 30 March 1977.

BRC&W-built No. 27033 slowly edges into the Scottish port town of Mallaig as it arrives at the end of its epic 165-mile journey with the 8.36 a.m. train from Glasgow Queen Street. The lucky passengers would have enjoyed one of the most scenic rides to be had on Britain's railways. 20 July 1977.

Life can be tough at the sharp end. On a bitterly cold day at Retford, a couple of PW staff get some welcome relief from their labours as a northbound HST passes. The hoped for Deltic in the snow never showed up that day. 17 February 1979.

Peak No. 44005 *Cross Fell* rolls out of Toton yard towards the site of the original Long Eaton station at around 6.30 p.m. on 7 July 1977. The ten Class 44s spent most of their lives working the heavy coal trains and a few days at this spot would usually bag them all.

Rarely seen in daylight towards the end of their careers, electro-diesel Class 74 No. 74004 stands at Woking with a Down parcels train in the early hours of 3 December 1977. The class was withdrawn by the end of the year, and this was likely to have been one of the last workings for this loco.

As a follow on to the previous shot, No. 74003 approaches Woking around 9 a.m. with a farewell tour to the 74s. Strangely enough I'd also snapped No. 74010 at Southampton in the early hours of the same day, so presumably Operations were giving drivers a nostalgic last run out on these locos for the memories! 3 December 1977.

There were often unexpected rewards for going off the beaten track and in this shot, framed by the gable end of the delightful overall roof at Beverley, an unidentified Birmingham RC&W Class 110 DMU approaches with a Scarborough–Hull service. 9 September 1976.

A spotter lurks in the shadows as Class 86 No. 86017 sweeps effortlessly through Nuneaton with a London Euston express during the heatwave and drought-stricken summer of 1976. The station was (and still is) a good place for freight, with Class 20s, 25s and 44s to be seen on the flyover line in the 1970s. 26 June 1976.

Class 47 No. 47232 drifts down towards Cardiff Central with a mixed freight. If I remember correctly the shot was taken from the footbridge leading to Cardiff Canton Depot, where any spotters of repute gathered to enjoy the daily freight-fest, and especially coal, that used to define the railways in these parts. 15 April 1978.

Lit by the floodlights at King's Cross, Deltic No. 55004 *Queen's Own Highlander* stands beneath the elegant roof with the 8.15 p.m. to Edinburgh (1S66). I was on my way to Waterloo and the SR for some overnight photography and happened to call in here on the off chance – I'm pleased I did now! 2 December 1977.

Taken on a family holiday to Mablethorpe in 1967, a visit to the station catches a Derby-twin Class 114 DMU waiting to depart with a service to Willoughby. My dad, then in his late thirties, is on the right looking on. Once part of the Great Northern system, traffic was already light and a network of lines, including this one, finally succumbed in 1970.

With the central gangway doors now removed and plated over, Sulzer No. 25080 coasts down the grade into the picturesque Bodmin Road station hauling a rake of hooded china clay wagons. The loaded train typically left Cornwall for The Potteries in the afternoon, and this is probably the return empties. 2 August 1979.

Peak No. 44002 *Helvellyn*, now without nameplates, stands at Toton Yard with the evening tanker trip working from British Celanese in Spondon. This was a reliable working for 44s and, arriving around 6.30 p.m., often prompted a bike ride with the camera on fine days. Taken from the busy A52 dual carriageway, it wasn't an outing for the faint-hearted. 20 May 1977.

BRC&W Type 2 No. 27043 passes the signal box at Mallaig Junction on the outskirts of Fort William with the 8.38 a.m. Glasgow Queen Street–Mallaig service. The train will reverse at Fort William before taking the line on the left to continue its journey. 19 July 1977.

Peak No. 45139 prepares to dive under Carrington Street Bridge and the Midland station concourse as it arrives into Platform 5 at Nottingham with a Midland Main Line service. It wasn't an especially long dive, but long enough for the guard to switch the carriage lights on when he remembered. 2 April 1977.

A fine day on the Woodhead Route sees 1,500 V DC electric No. 76003 negotiate the curve at Shorehall, near Penistone, with an eastbound freight. While it was good to see any Class 76 loco, the uncluttered fronts of those without the jumper cables facilitating multiple working were always a little more welcome. 20 June 1978.

The final day of Class 52 working was marked with a double-headed excursion, the 'Western Tribute', and this second shot captures the train passing through Bristol Temple Meads on its way to Plymouth with No. 1023 *Western Fusilier* and No. 1013 *Western Ranger* in charge. Loco No. 50037, a member of the class replacing them, can be seen to the right. 26 February 1977.

Captured at Attenborough, Class 37 No. 37040 hauls what is believed to be a train of imported steel billet from Grimsby/Immingham destined for one of the Black Country finishing plants. The elegant chalet-style station building was demolished in the early 1990s and the station is now unmanned. 5 July 1976.

Not the Western diesel-hydraulic I was desperately hoping for, but an as yet unnamed Class 50 No. 50003 does the honours as she bursts under the bridge at Teignmouth on to the sea wall section with an unidentified London Paddington express. 20 July 1976.

Framed by the ornate canopy supports of Middlesbrough station, and against a backdrop of cranes, Class 31 No. 31283 slowly makes its way past the Teesside dockyards with a rake of mineral wagons. 8 September 1976.

The then new order sees Doncaster-built Class 56 No. 56046 bowling down the Midland Main Line at Boots Bridge, Beeston, with a loaded MGR train bound for Ratcliffe-upon-Soar power station. The Nottingham city skyline can be seen at the top of the picture. 24 July 1979.

Snapped at Glasgow Central, one of the first generation WCML electrics, Class 81 No. 81003, departs with what is probably an ECS working. Sadly the locomotive caught fire in 1988 and the extensive damage, plus the by now non-standard nature of the class, resulted in her withdrawal. 26 Aug 1978.

The uniquely styled Swindon Inter-City Class 126 DMUs were exclusive to the Glasgow–Ayr/Stranraer routes when this shot was taken, and a visit to the area was made specifically to capture some of them on film. One such unit, with SC50936 leading, is pictured rolling into Newton-on-Ayr with a service from Glasgow. 30 August 1978.

The rural station of Reedham currently enjoys locomotive-hauled trains but in the 1970s DMUs ruled, as shown here where a Birmingham RC&W Class 104 approaches with a Norwich service. In a sign of the times the ballast is almost weedless, even on the passing loop, which doesn't look like it has seen a train in a while. 7 September 1976.

On a frosty, foggy day at the tail end of the year, 3-H Class 205 DEMU No. 1130 appears out of the gloom at Reading with a service from Basingstoke. 29 December 1976.

Determined to ride the west coast branch lines of Scotland as efficiently as possible, I travelled to Fort William and Mallaig, and then took the Thursday-only boat from Mallaig to Kyle of Lochalsh. This shot was taken the following morning and captures BRC&W-built Class No. 26032 waiting for its departure time with a train to Inverness. 22 July 1977.

Saltash station was never especially popular with photographers, but with its Great Western heritage and interesting backdrop a visit could be rewarding. Here a well turned out Class 50 No. 50047 eases through the station before crossing Brunel's Tamar Bridge with a Penzance–Paddington working. 3 August 1979.

The driver of Class 47 No. 47503 applies the power after slowing for the curve through Cheltenham Spa station with a north-east to south-west route service. The out of use Landsdown Junction Signal Box can be seen in the background. Of GWR heritage, it controlled the junction of the Midland and Great Western routes from Birmingham. 24 March 1979.

Woodhead electrics Nos 76006 and 76015 coast down the grade near Crowden with a rake of mineral wagons from the Yorkshire coalfield. While this rolling stock wasn't unusual, it nevertheless made a welcome change from the merry-go-round trains that featured heavily on the line and were used to supply the automated unloading facilities at Fiddlers Ferry power station. 1 June 1977.

Under the 1,500 V DC wires at Manchester Piccadilly, a pair of Class 506 three-car EMUs, led by M59608M, pull away with an afternoon service to Glossop and Hadfield. 8 November 1976.

Passing the rather careworn signal box, Peak No. 46015 slows for the curves through Rotherham Masborough station with a north-east to south-west route service. This now closed station was one of the best spots in the Sheffield area for watching the trains with both passenger and freight in plentiful numbers. 16 September 1977.

In the days when Severn Tunnel Junction was both a busy goods yard and stabling point, HST unit No. 253003 takes the London line with an early morning Cardiff–Paddington service. 15 April 1978.

A duo of Sulzers on the Midland Main Line. ETH-fitted Peak No. 45117, hauling a London St Pancras–Sheffield service, is seen racing past stationary Sulzer No. 25129, which is waiting for signals at Syston South Junction at the head of a ballast train. 8 June 1977.

A rare shot (for me) of a Class 84 captures No. 84002 resting up at Manchester Piccadilly after arriving with an ECS working on 15 November 1976. Designed by GEC and built in 1960 by the North British Locomotive Company, the ten locomotives were plagued with rectifier problems and were rarely entrusted with passenger trains in the 1970s.

Class 37 No. 37093 departs from Healey Mills yard with a rake of coal-laden mineral wagons in an everyday 1970s scene. Shiny rails and weedless ballast abound – in stark contrast to the scene of abandonment today and eerie sight of illuminated ground signals shining through the forest of small trees growing over the tracks. 30 March 1977.

A more artful capture sees a pair of Class 76s – Nos 76011 and 76014 – making seemingly easy work of the Woodhead grade as they whisk pass Wharncliffe Woods just north of Sheffield with a rake of MGRs destined for Fiddlers Ferry power station. 1 June 1977.

Another shot from the Castle Keep provides a wider view of Newcastle Central and captures Brush Type 4 No. 47053 snaking over the diamond crossings with the Haverton Hill–Leith ammonia tanks (6S41). The suburban platforms on the right were still in use and a pair of Metropolitan-Cammell units can be seen in the background. These platforms would eventually be deemed surplus to requirements and converted into a car park. 8 September 1976.

Exhaust fumes and leaking steam add to the atmosphere in the small hours at York station as Class 47 No. 47410 waits with a northbound East Coast Main Line service on 4 February 1978.

Arguably the most elegantly designed of all the first-generation DMUs were the Class 124 Trans-Pennine units built in 1960 at Swindon Works. Working a Hull–Liverpool train, one such unit calls at Huddersfield with motor coach E51966 leading. 12 April 1977.

When Royal Mail parcels and post still made for an important part of rail traffic, Class 86 No. 86255 pauses at Crewe and the gang get to work while the passengers board the train. Once numbered in their thousands and often a convenient seat for the visiting railfans, I still wonder where all the red mail trollies disappeared to! 4 March 1978.

Early in the season, and with the signal box apparently switched out, Class 47 No. 47090 *Vulcan* passes a damp Dawlish with a Down West of England express. While you can see where the nameplate should sit, I'm not entirely sure it was actually still attached to the loco at the time. 1 April 1978.

Peak No. 45132 whips up the snow as she passes through a wintry Beeston station with a London St Pancras–Sheffield service on 12 February 1978. The rail blue corporate branding of black letters on white background wasn't fully deployed here yet, seeing as the maroon LMR station sign was still in situ. I lived 400 yards away so I can't claim any suffering in snapping this.

On a summer's day in the 1970s, a family make the best of some unseasonably cool weather at Dawlish. In the meantime, and getting only a half-hearted response, Class 50 No. 50029 restarts its long train heading further west. This was the year of the heatwave but there was little sign of it here on this day. 18 July 1976.

In this shot, a week-long Eastern Region Rail Rover coupled with an overnight train from King's Cross provided for a dawn arrival in Newcastle, where first light catches a Class 03 shunter at the eastern end of the station, ready for the day's action. 6 September 1976.

Class 40s at Birmingham New Street were not too common in the 1970s so I probably struck lucky with No. 40102 on 10 September 1974. She lasted in traffic for little more than another year and was one of the first batch of the class to be withdrawn in early 1976.

A pair of Class 20s, with power applied, rattle over Trent South Junction at speed with a rake of covered mineral wagons. The locos are No. 20084, of Scottish origin judging by the cab recess for token equipment, and No. 20140. Seeing freight on the fast lines was quite rare, and it's possible this was an iron ore working from High Dyke routed through Nottingham. 7 May 1976.

The fine Caledonian station at Stirling makes an elegant backdrop to BRC&W-built Class 26 No. 26031, which is captured arriving with an unidentified service to Glasgow or Edinburgh. For me, those yellow snowploughs add some elegance to the class. 17 July 1977.

With the castle looming in the background Peak No. 45121 sets off from Nottingham with a mid-morning service to London St Pancras. The loco was one of a batch of fifty Peaks fitted with electric train heating equipment (denoted Class 45/1) to support the air-conditioned stock now used on the Midland Main Line. 3 September 1977.

Brightening up an otherwise dull day, Class 76 No. 76041 coasts down the Worsbrough Incline at Lewden Crossing with a mixed freight. This freight-only route linked the Yorkshire coalfield to power stations in the north-west and trains going up the 1 in 40 incline required banking. All traces of this scene are now long gone and the old route is now part of the national cycle network. 23 June 1977.

Once the largest marshalling yard in Europe, at its peak Toton handled a million wagons a year of mainly coal from the Nottinghamshire and Yorkshire coalfields. When this shot was taken the writing was already on the wall with the closure of a local ironworks and the introduction of merry-go-round wagon sets allowing coal to be moved direct from colliery to power station. 6 March 1977.

Against the splendid backdrop of the 'Auld Toun' in Edinburgh, split-headcode Peak No. 45025 waits time at Waverley station with a north-east to south-west route working. 18 July 1977.

The dainty Cravens Twin (Class 105) DMUs were mainly based in the east of England when this shot was taken and always seemed to attract a small but loyal fan base. Captured pulling away from Melton Mowbray with a Peterborough–Leicester service is set '37', comprising motor unit E50383 and driving trailer E56114. 1 October 1977.

Oozing with the atmosphere of the Great Western, the delightful wooden buildings at Lostwithiel station seem lost in a time warp as diesel-hydraulic No. 1053 *Western Patriarch* passes through with a china clay working. Both structures were eventually demolished and replaced by a brick booking hall, which itself is now surplus to requirements. 14 July 1975.

Fresh out of Doncaster Works, having been released only the day before, Deltic No. 55014 *The Duke of Wellington's Regiment* is seen approaching Doncaster with the 8.00 a.m. King's Cross–Edinburgh service (1S16), and is no doubt relishing some freedom after her four-month incarceration. 29 April 1978.

At Torside a pair of Class 76s – Nos 76011 and 76015 – make light work heading up the grade on the reverse curves towards Woodhead with a rake of empty MGRs heading back to the Yorkshire coalfield. Something of a last hurrah, the line closed five months later. 20 February 1981.

I was never a fan of prioritising loco haulage over photography, but when this one arrived at Perth behind a Class 25, and my next intended destination was Stirling, well I had to catch it. Of course it also meant a snapping opportunity on arrival, so here is No. 25068, working the 3.38 p.m. Dundee–Glasgow. 23 July 1977.

The signalman opens the crossing gates at Attenborough after passage of light engine No. 47199, seen disappearing into the distance – and it's obviously a warm day seeing as he's got the large window slid open. In the meantime the driver of the Morris 1800 has positioned himself to exploit the gap as soon as it becomes wide enough. 5 July 1976.

Still carrying a headcode panel, Peak No. 45139 takes the reverse curves through Manchester Victoria and opens up for the climb to Miles Platting with the 1.05 p.m. Pendleton–Topley Pike (6H34) empty aggregates. I've fond memories of The Coastal café on the platform opposite, which was always good for a greasy sausage roll and mug of tea. 16 September 1975.

By the date of this shot you could almost count on one hand the number of green-liveried Class 47s still to acquire their rail blue corporate overcoat. No. 47369, seen pulling into Platform 1 at Derby with a NE–SW route working, was to join the rail blue ranks a few months later. 9 July 1977.

On a bitingly cold day, Peak No. 45138 heads north through Wellingborough with a Midland Main Line service to Nottingham and Sheffield. The signalman at the south signal box was doing his job efficiently that morning, with the twin pegs already returned to caution before the last coach had passed. 10 December 1976.

Another shot from the picturesque Stirling station captures a three-car Metropolitan-Cammell DMU rolling into Platform 3 with a Sunday service to Edinburgh. Note the parcels and BRUTE trollies around the station, as well as the suitcase style of the day! 17 July 1977.

A trip to Dinting catches 1,500 V DC Class 76 No. 76053 crossing the viaduct into the station with a short but interesting freight, the 7.01 a.m. Northwich Yard–Whitemoor (8E67), on a misty late autumn day. I remember this as a regular morning runner having seen it a few times during trackside visits up there. 17 November 1977.

Peak No. 45128 approaches Boots Bridge, Beeston, with the 9.40 a.m. Sheffield–St Pancras, which had been diverted via Toton Yard. To the right is the Beeston Boiler Company, now gone and replaced by houses, and to the left is the siding serving Boots Company, which saw deliveries most days in the 1960s. 3 April 1977.

Class 40 No. 40063 makes a morning arrival into Inverness with the previous evening's 9.50 p.m. Royal Highlander sleeper service from London Euston. No. 40063 didn't have too long to rest up – she worked the 12.10 p.m. to Edinburgh a few hours later, which I took as far as Perth. 23 July 1977.

A pair of Class 76s – Nos 76026 and 76009 – leave the holding sidings at Wombwell Main and prepare to tackle the 1 in 40 graded Worsborough incline with a loaded MGR train. With a pair of bankers providing assistance, this was the only spot in the UK where you could regularly see four locomotives working the same train. 23 June 1977.

With just a Class 31 at his disposal, the driver of the 10.28 a.m. Taunton–Manchester Piccadilly train (1M72) lets common sense prevail and calls on the assistance of the Lickey bankers at Bromsgrove to help tackle the next two miles of 1 in 37.7 gradient. The engine is No. 31421 and the two bankers are Nos 37190 and 37223. 14 April 1979.

With mutual horn sounding the trio set off, this follow-up shot catches them working hard on the Lickey Bank itself. 14 April 1979.

Against a backdrop of cooling towers from the Ratcliffe-upon-Soar power station, Peak No. 45146 crosses the River Trent and eases for Trent South Junction with a Midland Main Line service to Nottingham and Sheffield. The bridge in the foreground crosses the Cranfleet Cut Canal. 7 May 1976.

In a typical summer morning scene at Exeter St Davids, when the splendid inner facade was still visible, No. 1025 *Western Guardsman* stands at Platform 2 with the 7.30 a.m. Paddington–Penzance service. In BR's questionable rush for standardisation, this locomotive was withdrawn in October 1975 when not quite twelve years old and with plenty of mileage still left in the tank. 1 July 1974.

Watched by a few enthusiasts, Class 47 No. 47402 heads a Down express through Grantham station. Only after I scanned this did I notice Dad carrying what looks like a microphone with wire leading to his Nutting Bag – presumably he was recording this to supplement his memories of the Deltics, or even No. 1023 *Western Fusilier*, which had passed earlier with the 'Western Talisman' excursion. 20 November 1976.

With palm trees scattered along the platform it could only be Cornwall, and this shot captures Class 50 No. 50018 *Resolution* pausing at St Austell with a Penzance–London Paddington service. The dock on the right was used for Motorail services from Kensington Olympia and Scotland. 30 July 1979.

Framed by the splendid GWR footbridge, Class 47 No. 47137 pulls into Bodmin Road station (now Bodmin Parkway) with what's believed to be the 10.20 a.m. Penzance–Leeds in the summer of 1976. With its sleepy nature, scenic location and the sounds of the signal box, summer visits here were always a pleasure. 21 July 1976.

Back to Shorehall Crossing, near Penistone, and this shot was taken of a Fiddlers Ferry power station-bound MGR train hauled by Class 76s Nos 76013 and 76012. These trains had a surprising turn of speed going up the incline and, with very little approach noise, it was easy to get caught unawares by them. 20 Jun 1978.

Under clear signals Deltic No. 55006 *The Fife and Forfar Yeomanry* demands attention as she hurries south through Retford with the 9.35 a.m. Newcastle–King's Cross service. Electrification and track realignment has changed this scene considerably, and the attractive Down platform buildings on the left are no longer there. 20 July 1974.

With the 1976 heatwave beginning to make its presence felt, Peak No. 45130 has the power on as she passes Beeston station with a St Pancras–Nottingham service. She'll be travelling around 80 mph just here and, with Nottingham just 4 miles away, will apply the brakes about a mile down the track. 5 July 1976.

Framed by the Caledonian signals, BRC&W-built No. 26032 heads towards Inverness station and its awaiting carriage stock, where it will form the 5.15 p.m. to Thurso and Wick. Thurso is as far north as the railway system goes in the UK, lying around 150 miles from Inverness and 700 miles from London. 22 July 1977.

In the early hours of a misty morning at Eastleigh, electro-diesel No. 73004 has just backed on to the 10.37 p.m. Weymouth–Waterloo mails to take the train through to London. The loco had arrived earlier with the 10.52 p.m. from Waterloo, which included parcels and passenger stock, and was notable for the fact that I occasionally managed to bag a cab ride! 18 February 1978.

On a quiet Tuesday afternoon, a single passenger waits at the quaint Dovercourt station in Essex for the train to Manningtree. Situated on the Harwich branch, the station is less than a mile from the Harwich Town terminus. 7 September 1976.

In the post diesel-hydraulic era, Class 50 No. 50048 *Dauntless* leaves Plymouth with a morning London Paddington-bound service. The patchy paintwork was something of a trademark on WR metals, which, rumour had it, was the result of over-zealous washing plants! July 1979.

Peak No. 45069 stands at Newcastle Central after arrival with a north-east to south-west route service. The stopover was generally a few minutes here and, if memory serves me right, the two chaps were the driver and secondman taking it on the next leg up to Edinburgh. 8 September 1976.

Another view of Wombwell Main Exchange Sidings catches a pair of 1,500 V DC electrics – Nos 76031 and 76032 – departing with a trainload of coal for Fiddlers Ferry. A couple of bankers will be assisting up the Worsborough incline behind me. The row of houses on Pearson Crescent would have had a grandstand view of the scene. 1 July 1977.

A visit to Marsh Junction in the early 1970s was generally rewarded with the sight of withdrawn diesel-hydraulics awaiting transfer to Swindon Works and the inevitable cutter's torch. This shot captures two of the eight that were there on this occasion, Hymeks Nos 7093 and 7055. 24 July 1973.

Lincoln St Marks was the terminus for the Crewe–Lincoln trains for many years, until construction of a new 80-metre rail connection enabled trains to be diverted to Lincoln Central, allowing St Marks station to be closed in 1985. The site now hosts St Marks Shopping Centre. 14 August 1975.

I know the sun is on the 'wrong' side (deliberately so I have to say), but this shot sums up the Woodhead Route for me – Bleaklow Hill of *Pennine Way* fame on the left and 1,500 V DC electric No. 76040 humming up the grade with a heavy freight of what looks to be scrap steel. Magic! 20 June 1978.

A relatively clean line-up at Hither Green Depot in South London comprises Class 73 No. 73001 and Class 33s Nos 33209 and 33053. The narrow body of the former, built to the Hastings line gauge, is clear in this shot. This photograph was taken when permission to wander around a BR diesel depot was more freely given. 20 March 1976.

Peak No. 44004, minus the *Great Gable* nameplates, drifts down into Toton Yard from the flyover line. The wagon repair shops are in the background and, while marshalling yard work was beginning to tail off, there was enough to keep three Class 08 shunters busy in this fairly limited view. 4 April 1979.

Another shot from Holmes Junction catches Peak No. 45137 *The Bedfordshire and Hertfordshire Regiment (T.A.)* shortly after leaving Rotherham Masborough with a north-east to south-west route express. With significant track rationalisation, together with vegetation growth, images from this spot are almost unrecognisable now. 16 September 1977.

Withdrawn even before it received the corporate blue livery, Hymek Class 35 No. 7054 is going nowhere fast in the scrapping lines at Swindon Works. 1 March 1975.

The 10.52 p.m. Waterloo–Southampton service was primarily a mail working but carried coaching stock for members of the public who wanted a late ride. A far better option was a ride in the cab, which I managed to wrangle on the odd occasion! The train is captured during its stop at Woking with electro-diesel No. 73134 in charge. 4 November 1977.

Snapped under the splendid Brunel roof at Bristol Temple Meads is HST unit No. 253027, which has arrived with the last train of the day from London Paddington. The train will head off shortly to St Philip's Marsh TMD, where it will be serviced and prepared for another day's work. 15 April 1978

Being under the 1,500 V DC wires at Mitchells Main in Yorkshire I was hoping for a Class 76 electric, but instead a clean-looking Class 40 No. 40147 shows up with what looks like an unfitted freight. I wasn't too disappointed! 23 June 1977.

Class 37 No. 37007 pulls into Dingwall with the 3.50 p.m. Invergordon–Inverness Yard (7N41) mixed freight. My Hakuba camera case and brown Adidas holdall (high fashion for all aspiring railfans) made a rare appearance in this shot – a happy bit of negligence on my part. 26 August 1978.

The signal box and gantry at Welsh's Bridge, Inverness, were high on the bucket list for any trip to the Highlands and captured here is Class 40 No. 40063 getting a clear run out of the station with the 6.55 p.m. to London Euston. 22 July 1977.

Hauling what's thought to be lime for the Steetley Works nearby, Class 37 No. 37160 gingerly takes the curve out of Hartlepool station beneath the floodlights of Victoria Ground, home to Hartlepool United FC. The guard has everything under control – his coat hung at his left and him sat on the right watching proceedings. 8 September 1976.

Peak No. 45148 powers up the slight gradient to Meadow Lane foot crossing, from Attenborough. The over-line conveyor belt of Trent Gravels forms the backdrop, and it is still there, albeit with a more contemporary look. Whether it will remain is open to question seeing as the site, now owned by Cemex, closed recently. 23 August 1976.

Bursting out of the tunnel and on to the Dawlish seafront is Class 50 No. 50015, as yet unnamed, with an unidentified eastbound express and rake of Mark 1 carriages. Despite it being a Saturday, nobody seems to be stirring on Marine Parade, although someone has been busy doing the washing. 1 April 1978.

In pre-electrification days, Deltic No. 55013 *The Black Watch* hurries the 9.52 a.m. Harrogate–King's Cross 'The Yorkshire Pullman' through Retford station. This stretch of the East Coast Main Line was still controlled by semaphores at the time, a few of which can be seen above the first carriage. 20 July 1974.

Back to the Woodhead Route and a pair of Class 76s – Nos 76016 and 76029 – coast down the grade at Wharncliffe Woods, just north of Sheffield, with what's believed to be the Stanlow Refinery–Ecclesfield petrol tanks working. 1 June 1977.

Snapped from a passing train at Truro, a lucky shot catches Class 52 No. 1040 *Western Queen* shunting cement wagons in the station yard, and I am nicely acknowledged by the driver. It was good to see a real headcode displayed, which is preferable to what was to become the habit of showing the loco number instead. 16 July 1975.

Sometimes even the mighty are called upon to do menial tasks. Deltic No. 55005 *The Prince of Wales's Own Regiment of Yorkshire* propels empty carriage stock into one of the bay platforms at Edinburgh Waverley while it awaits the arrival of the 10.35 a.m. Aberdeen–King's Cross 'The Aberdonian', which it will take on to London. 1 September 1978.

A damp day in Buxton yielded this shot, which shows Buxton Shed (9L or BX) with various motive power on display, the locomotives mostly assigned to the extensive quarry workings in the area. The platform curves away to the right, where the line (already removed) joined the old Midland Railway route to Bakewell. 15 November 1976.

Working a summer-timetabled 'Jolly Fisherman' from Derby to Skegness, a pair of Class 20s – Nos 20170 and 20037 – roll into Sleaford. This was a reliable turn for Class 20s, giving them a welcome change from their normal duty of moving coal from pithead to marshalling yard or power station. 13 August 1978.

More at home pounding the metals of the Midland Main Line, ETH-fitted Peak No. 45136 hauls a train of Mark 1 carriages along the coast at Dawlish. The position of the buffet car means a long walk for refreshments for anyone at the back of the train. 1 April 1978.

Built at Wolverton Works in 1960, the first member of the West Coast Main Line AM4s, No. 001, stands in the bay platform at Crewe with a service to Liverpool Lime Street. Limited to 75 mph, the units had a lively ride and the Gresley bogie, hardly cutting-edge technology in 1960, is clearly seen in this shot. 24 July 1977.

In the days when you could still ship a large carpet by train, Brush No. 47430 arrives at Huntingdon with a fast service to King's Cross. The flyover road in the background is the A14 Huntingdon bypass opened in the 1970s – it would be a challenge taking a contemporary shot that doesn't feature a heavy truck! 4 September 1976.

The 1 in 47 incline from Manchester Victoria up to Miles Platting, just over a mile from the city centre, could be a real challenge to freight trains, so a banking engine was usually left on standby ready to provide assistance. In this case, Sulzer No. 24024 is doing the honours. 19 August 1974.

With a rake of Mark 1 carriage stock in tow, Class 86 No. 86012 coasts down Shap with an Up express on 6 April 1979. In a testament to build quality, this locomotive is, as of 2018, still operational for Freightliner at over fifty years old, and is running as No. 86612.

With the signal off, the driver of Stratford-allocated Class 47 No. 47009 awaits the all-clear from the guard on a Liverpool Street–Norwich express at Colchester station. 7 September 1976.

The longest day was fittingly blessed with a fine evening and Grid No. 56017 is seen passing Trent South Junction with a rake of empty MGRs after emerging from Ratcliffe power station. With automatic unloading these trains didn't hang around. I'd snapped the loaded train passing Toton Yard just a couple of hours earlier. 21 June 1977.

With the help of a bus service between the two towns I managed to travel both spurs of the Thurso/Wick line from Inverness. Seen here at Wick in pretty dour weather is Class 26 No. 26025, ready to head back to Georgemas Junction, where it will join with the Thurso portion before returning to Inverness. 29 August 1978.

A Metropolitan Cammell Class 101 DMU rolls into Dunfermline with a service to Edinburgh lead by motor brake second SC51249. In a scene typical of the day, the guard already has his door open, surveying the scene for boarding passengers. 1 September 1978.

To accelerate the Glasgow–Edinburgh services, then handled by aging DMUs, a number of BRC&W Class 27s were converted to push-pull operation for work with specially modified rolling stock. The intensive 90-mph service would eventually take its toll on these locomotives. In the meantime, No. 27206 is seen here, having been diverted due to Sunday engineering work, while approaching Falkirk Grahamston with an unidentified unit on the back. 17 July 1977.

Class 47 No. 47503 passes Leicester North Signal Box and the impressive array of semaphores as she slows for the station with a Midland Main Line service to London St Pancras. 21 September 1979.

A late afternoon train to Exeter St Davids presented an unexpected window-hanging opportunity as we pulled into the station, where I was more than happy to see No. 1056 *Western Sultan* at Platform 1 with a Plymouth-bound parcels and BRC&W-built No. 33026 at Platform 2 with an already signalled passenger service to London Waterloo. 22 July 1976.

Peak No. 45146 approaches Leicester London Road, under clear signals, with a Sheffield–London St Pancras train on a sunny September day. The characterful backdrop of the Midland Railway warehouse, then used by National Carriers, is sadly now gone. 21 September 1979.

The Hartlepool station clock reads 9.25 a.m., and a two-car Metropolitan-Cammell Class 101 DMU stands in the bay platform with the 9.32 a.m. service to Darlington. 8 September 1976.

I barely remember seeing any freight trains at Edinburgh Waverley but I was lucky with this one and, even better, was in the right spot to snap it too. Class 47 No. 47298 eases the 12.45 p.m. Northfleet Cement Works–Uddingston View Park Blue Circle Terminal cement working (6S45) through the station. 9 March 1974.

Stripped of her nameplates and dignity, D1044 *Western Duchess* lies in Swindon Works, awaiting transfer to the breakers' yard. She ran 1.2 million miles in her short twelve-year life and, if the 1V38 headcode is good, she will have finished her duties working the 12.25 p.m. Birmingham–Paddington express – a nice way to sign off. 7 June 1975.

Captured during a heavy downpour and with windscreen wipers going, Class 50 No. 50012 *Benbow* passes through Par with an Up parcels train. These locomotives were viewed with suspicion by diesel-hydraulic lovers, with them having usurped their beloved machines, but were replaced themselves not many years later when HSTs were deployed on the West of England trains. 30 July 1979.

A resplendent Sulzer No. 25267 catches the evening sun as she approaches Beeston station with the 7.10 p.m. Nottingham–Crewe parcels train. On the days when it ran, the York Freightliner would be released as soon as this train cleared the section – something eagerly awaited by this photographer on sunny evenings! 5 August 1977.

Some six years before the Selby Diversion opened, effectively severing Selby from the East Coast Main Line, a pair of Class 37s – Nos 37018 and 37191 – head south through the elegant station with a rake of PTA iron ore tipplers. 19 November 1977.

Class 31 No. 31147 is captured passing through Brough station with a departmental train. At least as interesting are the unusual and lengthy shelters built to serve the commuting workforce of the Blackburn Aircraft Company factory (later Hawker Siddeley, and later still British Aerospace), which was located nearby. 9 September 1976.

In the days when health and safety rules were loose and a quick word with the foremen was often enough to get you unfettered access to the shed, a pair of Class 52s – Nos 1068 *Western Reliance* and 1067 *Western Druid* – stand on Long Rock Depot, Penzance, awaiting their next turns of duty. 25 May 1974.

Class 86 No. 86205 approaches Piccadilly station with the Down 'Manchester Pullman' train on 8 November 1976. Offering a premium service intended to capture business clients, the two rakes of Pullman carriages were based in Manchester and London respectively, each doing an out and back journey every weekday.

Getting the attention of a fellow snapper is Peak No. 46027 as it draws into Cheltenham Spa with a north-east to south-west route express. The platform furniture of the day in the form of BRUTES and Post Office trolleys adorn the station, together with GWR vintage seats, which I only noticed after scanning the slide. 27 August 1977.

Class 31 No. 31404 emerges from the 'City Widened Lines' at King's Cross with a train from Moorgate likely destined for the Hertford loop. Lifting a fully laden rush-hour train out of the station and up through Gasworks Tunnel proved quite a challenge for the Class 31s and invariably guaranteed plenty of engine thrashing! 7 September 1976.

Pulling away from Guide Bridge is a Class 506 EMU, with M59603M leading, with a train to Glossop and Hadfield. The station today is rather different, with just two platforms remaining (the two nearest the camera are now part of the car park) and little evidence of the thriving stabling point where Class 76s and Class 40s were guaranteed. 17 November 1973.

Kicking up the snow on New Year's Day is Peak No. 45147, which is seen approaching Boots Bridge, Beeston, with a Nottingham–St Pancras service. The locomotive met a grisly end in late 1984 while hauling a Liverpool–Scarborough service when she ran into a slow-moving oil tanker train at Eccles, sadly resulting in several fatalities. 1 January 1979.

Sulzer No. 25107 is captured heading a parcels train as she approaches Crewe. Such trains often comprised a variety of different vehicles and this is no exception: behind the locomotive is a GWR Siphon G, followed by a couple of BR GUVs and, further back, what looks to be a vehicle of SR origin. 4 March 1978.

Class 50 No. 50019 powers up through Dawlish with a London Paddington express. The locomotive was listed as being named *Ramillies* (after the Royal Navy battleship) in the 1978 Ian Allan Combine, so I'm guessing the nameplate was attached not too long after this shot was taken. 1 April 1978.

A group of railfans engage with the driver of Class 40 No. 40030 as he awaits the right away at Doncaster with an Up express. Originally named *Scythia*, the Class 40s lost their nameplates when relegated from regular express traffic. In this shot the original bolt holes can still be seen midway along the body. 14 June 1975.

On a day when conditions made you appreciate a F1.8 standard lens, one of the Farewell to the Class 24s tours, 'The Merseyside Express', is captured passing Hinkley, with locomotives Nos 24082 and 24133 both working hard. 14 January 1978.

Snapped approaching Clapham Junction is 4-SUB unit No. 4630 with a Waterloo–Shepperton service. Introduced in 1949, these units rarely strayed far from urban commuter territory and were already approaching the end of their working lives. Clapham Junction 'A' signal box is in the background. 17 February 1978.

Still in green livery, Class 40 No. 40039 leaves Healey Mills yard with an unfitted freight. One of the first batch of Class 40s to be withdrawn just over a year later, No. 40039 never did acquire the rail blue lick of paint. 22 July 1974.

A busy shot that, for me, captured the vibrant atmosphere at Guide Bridge. Sulzer No. 25270 heads east with a mixed freight as a couple of railwaymen walk towards the stabling point to sign on for the afternoon shift. The double-slip and points nearest the camera saw extensive use throughout the day as locos accessed and left the stabling point. 8 November 1976.

Deltic No. 55018 *Ballymoss* stands at King's Cross after arriving with the 'Hull Pullman'. With the steady roll-out of HSTs, the days were numbered for these East Coast Pullman sets. Balancing the shot are a couple of smartly dressed BR staff ambling down the platform, polished black shoes noted! 17 February 1978.

Deep in rural Cornwall, the driver of D1053 *Western Patriarch* makes a slow pass-by at Lostwithiel Crossing Box in order to collect the single line token for the Fowey branch with a returning rake of empty china clays. 14 July 1975.

The first week of July was gloriously sunny and on four of the five nights the British Celanese tanks were Class 44 hauled. Suffice to say, home from work and after a quick bite, it was time to cycle off to Long Eaton to catch, on this occasion, No. 44005 (ex-*Cross Fell*) doing the honours around 6.30 p.m. 5 July 1977.

Having worked up to Hull earlier in the day, Deltic No. 55018 *Ballymoss* heads back south through Newark with the 12.34 p.m. Hull–King's Cross train. Hull services benefitted from the cascaded Deltics for a while, but they were on borrowed time and the last Deltic-hauled service train ran in December 1981. 16 May 1981.

If the Class 26s don't date this shot, then the Hillman Avenger probably does. BRC&W units Nos 26015 and 26022 pull into Inverness with a train from the south during the fine late afternoon of 22 July 1977.

This shot was taken at Southminster terminus after catching the local cart from Wickford. Being a Sunday I took the same train back to avoid being stranded, but I did have time to bag a couple of images, and this one shows the train signalled for the return journey; the BRC&W trailer unit is E59243. The driver is just returning from the signal box, presumably having registered the single line token collected at Fambridge on the way out. The branch is now electrified and forms an important commuter link into Central London for folks who prefer the quieter, more rural life. 5 September 1976.